The Question to Everyone's Answer:

How to Stay Motivated on a Daily Basis

David A. Rich

Illustrations by: Marty Unger

KENDALL/HUNT PUBLISHING COMPANY
4050 Westmark Drive   Dubuque, Iowa 52002

Copyright © 1994 by David A. Rich

Library of Congress Catalog Card Number: 94-77886

ISBN 0-8403-9849-2

Printed in the United States of America
10 9 8 7 6 5 4 3 2 1

CONTENTS

THE SUSTAINERS

FOREWORD

Motivation has been the centerpiece of David's entire business career. He was fired from his first sales job for lack of it. He prospered in his second sales position because he had it. He built a successful speaking business during the recession with no start up capital because he could maintain it. In fact, in the past five years since I met David, I would be hard pressed to think of anyone who has been more motivated. While all of us hopefully are able to capture our fair share of motivation, it has always baffled me how some, like David, can command it.

There are books that can teach you to do just about anything you'd like to do, anything your heart desires. But where is the book on how to get your heart to desire, and then keep it that way? You can indeed be whatever you want to be, and do whatever you want to do, but before all that being and doing, you must have motivation. Motivation separates the men from the boys, the have's from the have not's. Being able to control your own motivation is the ultimate success.

Here is your chance. Finally a complete book on getting and staying motivated, for whatever you want from your life. It contains no secrets or earth-shattering revelations, just simple, practical methodology to build and sustain your own reservoir of motivation. Great things await your action. I'm sure he wouldn't mind me stealing the words he has so often proclaimed to his audiences—"Motivation is the heart of all success."

Patrick J. Dunstan
National Sales Training Manager
United States Chamber of Commerce

INTRODUCTION

You've heard of answers to questions, but probably never questions to answers. Nevertheless, that's what this book is all about. We all want different answers to our lives. Talk to one hundred people, you'll get almost one hundred different answers as to what they want out of life. For some it may be a new house, car, or other material possession. For others a new job or career. Maybe the answer is in losing weight, getting in shape, or taking a class or two. Some want to travel, read more, relax more or learn a musical instrument. Or maybe it's just to be a better person, parent or friend.

But no matter what our individual answer is, the question is the same for each of us: How do we stay motivated on a daily basis to achieve our answers? Yes, I did say "daily." Staying focused, energetic, and enthusiastic is a day-to-day proposition. Unfortunately, motivation can not be saved or stored up for use at another time.

We all are guilty of suffering from the disease I call "motivation fluctuation." Some fluctuation is inevitable and cannot be avoided, but it is also no coincidence that those who seem to achieve the most are those who have learned to control their rate of fluctuation.

One way is to build a strong "motivation foundation." Let's see how strong your foundation is. Here's a test.

1. How often does your motivation fluctuate? Daily, hourly, minute to minute?

2. Do you experience sudden, sometimes even unwanted, bursts of energy? And then, conversely, are there times when you just can't get motivated no matter what. You know what I mean: couch potato time.

3. Does your motivation seem out of your control?

4. Can outside influences affect, or even take away your motivation?

5. Does your mood affect your actions?

6. Do you ever wish you were motivated, but have nothing to be motivated for?

If you answered "yes" at least once, the question of how to stay motivated applies to you. Motivation is a daily, if not hourly, challenge. It is the greatest challenge we face. It's the question to our answer, whatever it is. And it's one thing to get motivated, another to stay that way. So it is written that "some people are motivated for thirty minutes, some others for thirty days. But it is the person who is motivated for thirty years who is truly successful."

But that's easier said than done. How exactly do you stay motivated on a daily basis? Well, stay tuned. You've come to the right place. The quest for motivation is a journey, and the journey begins now!

Setting The Stage

◆▶ ◆▶ ◆▶ ◆▶ ◆▶ ◆▶

CHAPTER

The Myths About Motivation

ONE

66 **S**uccess is going
from failure to failure
without losing
enthusiasm. 99

WINSTON CHURCHILL

Motivation. There are few words that are as misunderstood as that one. Misconceptions about what motivation is and how it works are responsible for many shattered dreams.

You see, we all have dreams. Dreams come in many shapes and sizes and are referred to by several different names. Plans, hopes, aspirations, goals, intentions, and desires are all forms of dreams. Having dreams is as basic to human nature as survival. Man is the only living creature able to dream. This is truly a powerful distinction.

But what happens to our dreams? How about the wild, wacky, fun kind of dreams we had as kids? You remember, the ones about turning invisible, sword fighting the bad guys, living in a castle, flying through the air on the back of a dragon, etc. Those are fantasy dreams, dreams that were never really intended to come true. Just fun, innocent imagination. We didn't really abandon those fantasies, we simply grew out of them.

Then there are aspiration dreams, dreams of what we want to be when we grow up. There are no age restrictions here: many adults are still looking for that answer. We may dream of being a movie star, baseball player, doctor, the President. We dream of places we'll go, things we'll have, projects we'll complete.

These dreams have a chance. These dreams most definitely can come true. We don't grow out of these dreams; unfortunately, we just let them die. Oh, certainly not by design. We start to think we're too old, too poor, too unfortunate, too uneducated, or too stuck in our ways. We let past failures get in the way. Some people reach the point where it is less painful not to dream, than to suffer another defeat. After all, some say, dreams are just kids' stuff.

Where did we go wrong? What happened to believing that we could achieve whatever we wanted? What happened to the enthusiasm and motivation we had as kids?

It is said that the world is divided between dreamers and do-ers. But I don't believe this is quite true. There are actually three categories. Those who just dream and never do, those who dream and do, and those who have lost their dream.

The prescription for all three is MOTIVATION. Motivation is the inner mechanism that prompts us to take action. Dreams plus action equal achievement. Dreams with no action lead to the loss of our dreams. But motivation is not easy. There are many challenges. How do you get motivated? And just as important, how do you stay motivated? And why does motivation get harder, not easier, the older we get?

Maybe we don't really understand what motivation is or how it works. Or maybe we have found it easier to buy into the common myths about motivation. Let's examine the four common motivation myths so there is no misunderstanding about what motivation is.

MYTH #1

MOTIVATION IS AN EFFECT, NOT A CAUSE

Remember when you were little and still believed in Santa Claus, did you wait until Christmas Eve to get excited about Christmas? Or did it begin several weeks in advance? Around Thanksgiving? Halloween? Maybe even a week after last Christmas? That's motivation! Unfortunately, we get trapped into believing the myth that motivation is an effect, not a cause. The truth is *motivation*

66 The real secret
of success is
enthusiasm. **99**

WALTER CHRYSLER

always happens in advance of something good. Not the other way around. Motivation is a cause, not an effect. Somewhere along the way we began to wait until something good happened to us before we got excited and motivated. The problem is that this is a "Catch 22". We're not motivated because nothing good or motivating is happening, and nothing good or motivating is happening because we're not motivated. There's no magic about it. Motivation is a pay-first proposition. Motivation is the cause of great things, not the result of them.

MYTH #2
YOU CAN'T CONTROL MOTIVATION

Most people believe that motivation is external, not internal, something outside of our direct control. Other things, circumstances, and people determine our motivation levels. The truth is *all motivation is self motivation.* Motivation is an internal decision, not an external result. The premise that motivation is a decision is the core belief behind this book. Motivation is nothing more than a choice.

Through my years of experience as a sales trainer, I've come across a countless number of extremely talented salespeople who never quite lived up to their potential. The problem was not in their skill level, it was their motivation level. By their own admission, staying motivated, enthusiastic, and focused was their downfall.

I'd ask them what would motivate them. The common replies were things like making a sale, recognition, or a large commission. Good things for a sales person to be motivated by. Then I'd ask if those rewards were in their control. Most admitted they were. The next question would be what specific activities could they engage in that could lead to those results. As soon as they began to list activities, they began to feel motivated and empowered. They themselves held the key to motivation, without ever knowing it. The choice was their own.

The first step is recognizing that we can control motivation. It is a choice. But behind any choice is action. You can only eat an elephant one bite at a time. Action, no matter how small, is the first step in getting motivated. (P.S. You've already taken the first step by buying this book.)

Myth #3

Motivation is Just Fluffy Stuff

As a speaker, I hear this all the time. Clients want skills, they don't just want motivation. After all, motivation is just fluff.

What they fail to realize is that without motivation, the skills are useless. Knowledge is important, but acting on the knowledge is what counts. And action requires motivation. But this myth goes deeper than just acting on skills. *I believe motivation is a skill in itself.* It is not merely a supplement to knowledge, it *is* knowledge.

It's one thing to teach a skill motivationally; it's another to teach the skill of motivation. That's why I cringe when people refer to this book as motivational. Not that I wouldn't want it to be inspiring, but this book is intended to be a "how to" guide on getting and staying motivated—very specific, nuts and bolts, down and dirty. These are not traditionally words associated with motivation. Before you go any further in this book, please accept the fact that motivation is a learned activity and that it's never too

66 F<small>all</small> down
seven times,
stand up eight. **99**

J<small>APANESE</small> P<small>ROVERB</small>

late to learn it. Motivation is the mother of all skills. It is the horse before the cart.

MYTH #4

MOTIVATION IS ONLY NECESSARY AT CERTAIN TIMES

Motivation is too often the exception to the rule, rather than the rule itself. It is used frequently to describe someone who's on the rise. A go-getter. A star on the horizon. Someone on a mission. More often than not, it is business people we're referring to. They've got a reason to be motivated. The truth is they have no more reason to be motivated than anyone else. Motivation, or lack of it, is extremely non-discriminating.

The common myth is that motivation is only necessary for those times when we are facing great challenges, climbing the mountains, slaying the dragons, attempting big things. Although those undertakings require motivation, the real tests of motivation do not take place in the marketplace or on an athletic field or in a board room, but rather in the private seclusion of our homes. *Motivation is about everyday life.* Facing ordinary tasks with vigor, finding the strength to get out of bed each morning, fighting procrastination, and staying positive are a few of the less than glamorous battles we fight everyday. These are the real tests of motivation.

Winston Churchill once wrote that "success is going from failure to failure without losing enthusiasm." The late Dr. Norman Vincent Peale said, "Those people who consistently live with motivation and enthusiasm seem to have a remarkable mastery over circumstance."

Motivation and enthusiasm shape the quality of our lives, no doubt about it. But it's not easy, and no one person or occupation has the corner on motivation. It is a daily proposition. Yesterday's motivation is no good to us today. It's about time we acknowledge its importance—everyday!

These are not the only myths about motivation. Another common misconception is that money cures all motivation problems. While I do admit money can be motivating in the short term, it is proven to be only temporary. *Motivation is not a result of having money, it is the other way around.* Motivation is a cause. If we accept this, we are no longer victims of fate, but rather creators of our own destiny. We can and must control our own thinking, and thus our own levels of motivation and enthusiasm. We hold the power, the secret to success, internally. This is not just self-help, feel-good, fluffy stuff. Self motivation is a tangible, learnable skill. A skill that translates into quality of life. A skill that is necessary for all of us.

Getting and staying motivated is a uniquely universal challenge. Unique, because each of us wants different things out of life. What would you like to be more motivated for? What do you want for your life? More money, a house, a car, prestige, a family, peace of mind, an exciting career, or just to live with more enthusiasm and zest? What is your "what"?

And do you know *why* you wish for the things you wish for? I can give you the how to's, but the what's and the why's have to come from you. If you're not sure, take heart. I'll give you some help developing your dreams in Chapter Five. Our what's and why's are our exclusive property. They're like our fingerprints. Every one of us has our own what's and why's. There are as many answers to life as there are people.

The Human Race

Whatever your answer, the question remains the same for all of us. How do we stay motivated enough to get what we want? And not just motivated here and there, but every day, consistently. This brings us full circle. I assume that's why you're here. This book contains no magic formula, and no real earth-shattering secrets. Just simple, practical, and effective techniques to help you stay motivated to find your answers in life. Warning: changing the way you think and act is required. Open your mind to new ideas and it may never be the same again. Fair enough? Let's begin!

66 Many of life's
failures are people who
did not realize how close they
were to success when
they gave up. **99**

THOMAS EDISON

CHAPTER

Changing
The Way
You Think

TWO

The starting point for getting and staying motivated is to actually change the way we think. Motivation begins and ends with *how* we think. Most of us think, and thus live each day, as if the motivation myths of Chapter One are truths. To the extent that we believe each particular myth, the more deeply rooted it is in our subconscious. When a belief gets deeply rooted in our subconscious, our actions become instinctual, which then form habits.

When we think of habits, we think of physical habits, or actions. But not all habits are physical. We have thinking habits as well. I call these thinking habits "thinkmodes." Thinkmodes are the foundation of our belief system. They can either be positive or negative. Our positive thinkmodes are a constructive force in our lives, while negative ones can be extremely self limiting. The reason some people see a glass as half empty instead of half full is a result of a negative thinkmode. They habitually see the world through negative eyes, and in return get labelled as pessimists. Conversely, successful people have positive thinking habits.

We tend to repeat our thinkmodes millions of times in a single lifetime. So the first step is to take inventory of our thinking habits, and if necessary, reverse our negative thinkmodes. This, of course, is a lot easier said than done. If habits were not hard to reverse, we'd have more people quitting smoking, staying on diets, and exercising regularly, etc. Old physical habits, and thinkmodes, are indeed extremely hard to reverse. My advice: don't even try. Trying to reverse a habit can lead to stress and depression that eventually reinforces the habit.

Instead of reversing a physical habit or thinkmode, replace it! For physical bad habits, replace them with other, more positive activities. That sounds easy, but the willpower necessary to do that comes from the thinkmode connected to the activity. For

66 There is no
security, only
opportunity. **99**

GENERAL MACARTHUR

instance, if it brings you more pleasure to smoke than grief not to smoke, it will be virtually impossible to replace that activity. The dominant thinkmode is the joy associated with smoking, rather than the ill effects it can bring. Tony Robbins, famous author and speaker puts it this way: "What you *link* pain and pleasure to ultimately shapes your destiny." Remember the word *link*. I will refer to it again in Chapter 8. You'll need to replace negative thinkmodes with positive, empowering thinkmodes. Let me give you a few simple techniques to help you do this and condition your thinking for maximum motivation. In short, to change the way you think.

The Art of Beginning

Begin by committing to change. Whatever your desired result, take some kind of action toward it, regardless of how insignificant it may seem. The hardest step is always the first one. Remember the NIKE slogan, "Just do it." Sometimes too much thinking about something will lead to self doubt and result in procrastination and lowered motivation.

Dr. Steven Covey in his much-heralded bestseller, *The Seven Habits of Highly Effective People*, suggests to "Begin with the end in mind." Focusing on the end result makes it easier to begin. Motivation feeds off momentum and action, and momentum needs a beginning. Motivation is first a decision, then a feeling.

The first step is to make the decision to live your life with more enthusiasm and motivation. Edward Butler once wrote that "some people have enthusiasm for thirty minutes, others for thirty days, but it is the person who has it for thirty years that is truly successful." Make the decision right now to get and stay more motivated. Sounds simple. It is. Not easy, but simple. Congratulate yourself, you've just begun!

Immediate Gratification

Actually, congratulating yourself has a hidden purpose other than the obvious. Small, seemingly insignificant forms of immediate gratification, such as congratulating yourself, can help kindle the flame of motivation.

Immediate gratification has gotten a bad rap through the years. We're constantly told to delay gratification. While it is good to delay the bigger, ultimate rewards, withholding all rewards unfortunately also handicaps motivation. To sustain high levels of motivation requires constant positive reinforcement. Reward yourself often along the way with small things, like a dinner out, a self-made banner, or even a calendar with gold stars on it. Hey, it works for children; it can work for adults too.

We've been conditioned to dismiss smaller rewards as insignificant. Yet they play a major role in the development of your motivation level. Let your motivation build on small victories. This is a change in the way we normally think. Most people get so obsessed with the end result, that they neglect any progress they might make along the way.

The "Think As If" Technique

As you reward and encourage yourself for your progress, there is a tendency to get complacent. The "think as if" technique is a simple one that can help keep you on track. We all have an ideal

66 They always
say that time changes things,
but you actually
have to change them
yourself. **99**

ANDY WARHOL

self, or self-ideal which is the person we would like to be. Simply "think as if" you already were that person. Let your self-ideal govern your thought process. When faced with a decision or challenging situation, ask yourself this question: How would the person I'd like to be respond to this situation? What decision would that person make?

This simple technique of considering your ideal self can help make any decision easier to make. Apply this technique any time you think or act differently from the way your ideal self would think or act.

Have you noticed that we need motivation the most when it is hardest to get motivated? For example, first thing in the morning. Studies show that first thing in the morning is when our minds are most alert and our thinking is clearest. Yet how many of us find it a chore just getting out of bed? Or how about when we find ourselves with that endless list of things to do, and not enough time to do them? How do you react? Do you get depressed? Do you complain? It is at times like these that we most need to remember the "think as if" technique.

Thinking as if is a form of mental conditioning that I will refer to again and again. It is the internal component necessary for staying motivated. Thinking as if is the habit that leads to mental imaging and mental rehearsal, which is the ability to play something out in the mind before it happens physically. Studies on Olympic athletes have proven that practicing mentally is just as effective as practicing physically. Mental imaging, rehearsing, and thinking as if are crucial in the battle to stay motivated on a daily basis. Earl Nightingale once sold more records than anyone previously when he released a fifteen minute monologue titled, *The Strangest Secret in the World*. He proclaimed, "We become what we think about." Our thoughts become our actions, our actions become us. Think as if you already are the motivated person you want to become.

But thinking as if is not enough. You'll need actions to support your thinking. You'll need "SOMA POWER."

"Soma Power"

The final step in conditioning your thinkmodes for optimum motivation is to learn how to tap into what I call "SOMA POWER," which is short for *somapsychotics*. This is the physical manifestation of the "think as if" technique. If you're scratching your head wondering what that is, let me explain. You're probably already familiar with a related word, psychosomatics. The word psychosomatic is most commonly used to refer to psychosomatic illnesses. However, contrary to popular belief, the word psychosomatic does not mean imaginary, just as a psychosomatic illness is not an imaginary illness. It merely means it originated in the mind. The root word psycho means mind, the word soma means body. Put together, the word psychosomatic means that something starts in the mind first, body second.

Have you ever said out loud, or to yourself, that you're beginning to feel sick, or that you hope you don't get sick? That is psychosomatic. Your mind has recognized the sickness before your body has.

This is not, however, just reserved for illnesses. In fact, most people live the majority of their lives psychosomatically. When we think of depressing things, our bodies react with a frown. When we hear something funny, we laugh. When we think of something pleasing, we smile. All are examples of psychosomatics, bodily actions that originated in the mind. In short, most people let their thoughts dictate their actions.

I once had a salesperson come into my office announcing she was depressed. She slumped into a chair, spoke barely above a whisper, and wore a frown on her face. My initial reaction was "of course you're depressed." Her mind had registered the depression and her body followed suit. She was the perfect candidate for *Somapsychotics.*

"Somapsychotics" is putting actions before thoughts. It is the exact opposite of mind over matter. This is matter over mind—changing our thoughts by changing our physiology.

Changing your body language is easier than changing your thoughts. For example, instead of her sitting slumped in a chair, dwelling on negative things, I had her get up and MOVE <u>as if</u> she was not depressed. It was hard at first, because her mind was not into it, but with some prodding she was able to let her actions cure her depression. You can clap your hands, pump your fists, smile, laugh, cheer, yell, read something positive, or listen to your favorite song. You get the picture. Matter over mind.

Remember that thinkmodes are habits of thinking, and like all habits, they take time and discipline to develop. Studies show that it takes twenty-one days to form or break a habit twenty-one days in a row, consistently, without fail.

So, let's combine a few techniques we've already learned. Begin by committing to live with more motivation and enthusiasm. Start small, with just the next twenty-one days. Reward yourself after every three days. Use "soma power" to help you when the going gets tough.

Building the Foundation

In the next four chapters, we will discuss the elements that help build a solid "motivation foundation." Motivation requires a strong foundation, which can be built. For this reason, I compare it to construction. Every good construction worker knows that a structure is only as good as its foundation. To build a strong foundation, there are certain steps to take, and certain steps to avoid. It's the same with motivation. Some things help build, others destroy. The positive thinkmodes I call "motivation builders." The negative thinkmodes are "motivation zappers." As you read about each one, take a personal inventory. Ask, "Is this true for me? To what extent?" If it's zapping your motivation, ask "How can I turn this into a builder?" You may need to change the way you think!

66 The hand
is the cutting edge of
the mind. **99**

JACOB BRONOWSKI

2 THE MOTIVATION FOUNDATION

THE BUILDERS & ZAPPERS

CHAPTER

Negativity

THREE

66 You can't
build a reputation on what
you're GOING
to do. **99**

HENRY FORD

Motivation needs a solid foundation. The strength of the foundation determines how much "motivation fluctuation" we experience on a regular basis. And to make matters worse, the foundation can change in different situations. With some activities and situations our foundation may be strong, with others it can be very weak. That's why staying motivated is so hard, and why no one can live without experiencing some motivation foundation fluctuation. The question is not, do we fluctuate, but rather how often and how much fluctuation is there? And what do we do when our motivation does fluctuate? What impact does that have on our attitude?

In this chapter, and the next three, we will begin to explore the effects of the factors that build up (builders) and that tear down (zappers) our motivation foundation. Interestingly enough, each factor can be either a builder or zapper. For example, the first factor is *negativity*. High negativity is a zapper, low negativity is a builder.

There are two forms of negativity, external and internal. Let's address external negativity first, because it is more identifiable than its internal counterpart.

External Negativity

External negativity is negativity that comes from tangible things outside of us, such as people, places, events, television shows, etc. This is why it is more often than not a zapper. It originates outside of ourselves, thus reducing the amount of direct control we have over it.

Negativity cannot be totally eliminated, but it can be held in check. Negativity, in check, becomes a builder of motivation.

The correlation between negativity and motivation is a simple one. Negativity lowers energy. It is estimated that the average person's life contains ten times more negative input from external sources than positive input. Whether the ratio is actually ten to one is irrelevant. There is little doubt the negatives outweigh the positives.

Just turn on your local news. Any good news gets lost in a barrage of bad. And society continues to tune in. Negativity, unfortunately, seems to sell. The more negative the evening news, the higher the ratings. This alarming trend can end, but only when we as a society make the decision to stop tolerating it.

The effects of external negativity are like a cancer. Sometimes we don't realize those effects until it is too late. Studies show that the average American falls asleep at night during or right after a news broadcast. What's damaging about this is that our subconscious mind does not sleep. It continues to work on whatever input it received last. The quality of the input is indiscernable to our subconscious. Whatever input goes into our conscious mind filters through to our subconscious mind, and it is our subconscious mind that controls the majority of our thoughts, feelings, actions, and motivation. Simply put, negative in, negative out.

Studies have concluded that there is a definite link between what people do before falling asleep and how they feel when they wake up. Those people who fall asleep with positive input, such as an inspirational book or audio, wake up feeling more refreshed and energetic. Positive input is revitalizing, while negative input is taxing and psychologically draining.

Although it is relatively easy to control what you choose to watch on TV, or what you do before falling asleep, it gets stickier when it comes to negative people. Negative people are those who seem to thrive on bringing others down, either by *criticizing, complaining,* or *condemning.* I call them "triple C" people. They perpetually see the glass as half empty, instead of half full. Triple C people can be found all around us. It is imperative to our quest for higher levels of enthusiasm and motivation for us to minimize our time around negative people. The C's are highly contagious. If you have to spend time with triple C people, be sure not to add fuel to their fire. Don't play along, or join in their misery. Let them know in no uncertain terms that negativity has no constructive purpose in your life. Remember, the power of life lies in the choices we make. Choose not to allow negative people to affect you. External negativity must be held in check or it can become internalized.

Internal Negativity

Internal negativity comes from intangible things inside of us. We can walk away from negative people, or turn off negative TV shows, or avoid negative surroundings. But when the negativity comes from internal sources, we are stuck. Unlike external negativity, we cannot just simply walk away. We have to face this form of negativity head on.

Just as the triple C's can be found in external people, they can be found internally as well. Who do you think talks to you more than anyone else? If you said yourself, you're right. Even though it's not out loud, we talk to ourselves all the time through our thoughts. Thoughts are self communication. Unfortunately, most self talk is negative. The most common self talk is things like: I don't feel good, I'm too tired, I'm too old (or too young), I'm too poor, I don't like my job, I hate rainy days, etc. etc.

66 **O**pportunity is
missed by most people
because it is
dressed in overalls and
looks like work. **99**

THOMAS EDISON

Most of us are unaware that there is a direct correlation between what we say to ourselves and how we feel about ourselves. Flip Wilson used to say, "What you see is what you get." The more accurate statement would be, "What you *say* is what you get." Our self communication is a barometer of how we feel about ourselves. People with higher levels of self esteem have more positive self talk, and those with lower esteem have more negative self talk.

The truth is it's a vicious cycle. The more negative our self talk, the worse we feel. The worse we feel, the more negative the self talk. The cycle must and can be broken.

Remember that it takes only twenty-one days to form or break a habit. So for the next twenty-one days in a row, engage in only positive self talk. When you catch yourself saying something negative, stop yourself and say something positive instead. The negative thought will still probably be in the back of your mind, that's ok. Fake it till you make it. The drill of saying positive things will eventually erode the negative thought.

We've already determined that whatever you put into your conscious mind filters into your subconscious mind. Your subconscious mind only knows what you tell it. It's like a computer. It doesn't know the difference between the real and the imagined. So program it with positive input. Do the same thing when you find yourself worrying about something. Worrying holds the negative thought in your conscious mind, thus allowing the thought to plant firmly into your subconscious. And anything that gets rooted in your subconscious, good or bad, has a greater chance of happening. That's why it is important to make sure only positive input makes it to your subconscious. Sometimes you'll need to pull an acting job on your mind. Start saying the positives to yourself. If a few slip out loud, all the better. Saying things out loud speeds up the filtration to the subconscious.

What to do When You're Down

Everyone gets down. What's damaging is not the fact that you're down, it's how long you're down. The longer you stay depressed, the harder it is to pull out of it, and the consequences may be greater. When you're down, it means something negative made it to your subconscious. This is when you'll need the power of positive words the most. Proclaim the good things in your life.

As bad as things sometimes get, they can almost always be worse. In Og Mandino's classic, *A Better Way To Live*, he suggests you take inventory of the blessings in your life. Are you handicapped? Do you live in pain? Do you live in fear for your life? Are you without your eyesight? Is your body not whole? Are you deprived of your freedom? Are you unable to exercise your greatest freedom, the power to choose? We must learn the difference between problems and mere inconveniences.

Even if you do have one of the aforementioned challenges, you still posess the power to conquer and control it, and not let it conquer and control you. The decision to live life positively or negatively is ours to make. We must make this decision daily, many times over. The greatest of all freedoms is the ability to choose our emotions. This is the ultimate success. Yet very few people regularly exercise this right. View it as a battle. The negative forces versus you. Who's going to win? It's not easy. It's a never-ending battle. But it's still your choice.

66 The only way to
avoid being miserable is
not to have enough leisure time
to wonder whether you
are happy or not. **99**

GEORGE BERNARD SHAW

A Final Thought About Negativity

External and internal negativity are a part of life. They'll never go away. We can't eliminate them. We can only control their effects on our life. It's like the person who is trying to lose weight. He or she can't control the quantity of desserts and junk food in the world. But that person can control what goes into his or her own body. It's a matter of will power.

As with the person who is trying to lose weight, it is equally important how you react to momentary bouts of negativity. The dieter gets ashamed and depressed about giving in to the urges. Beating up on yourself will only weaken your resolve and lead to more frequent indulgences. Accept what has happened is past; you no longer have control over it. Learn from the experience. By not dwelling on a momentary lapse, you will strengthen your resolve, and thus decrease the odds of repeating it.

Periodic doses of negativity are inevitable. They help keep us humble and appreciative. There's a good in every bad. Look for the silver lining. Look for ways to do things better. Learn from every experience, and you'll be on your way to a more positive and motivated life. That's the idea!

66 Take a music
bath once or twice a week,
you will find that it is
to the soul what the water bath
is to the body. **99**

OLIVER WENDELL HOLMES

CHAPTER

Self Esteem

FOUR

The second "builder and/or zapper" is *self esteem*. Self esteem is not as obvious as negativity. Many people suffer from low self esteem without even realizing or admitting it. High self esteem builds our motivation foundation; low self esteem zaps it. Let's start off by defining self esteem. Many people confuse self esteem with self image. Self image is the way you think others see you. Self esteem is the way you *feel* about yourself. Self esteem, like many feelings, is connected to motivation through the subconscious mind. The better we feel about ourselves, the more likely we are to stay motivated. It's that simple. So let's look at some things that lower self esteem, and those that raise self esteem.

SELF ESTEEM ZAPPER #1
BLAME

Blame is the first of what I refer to as useless emotions that kill self esteem. Blame serves no constructive purpose. It is an after-the-fact emotion. If blaming could change the circumstances, I'd be the first to say, do it. But it can't. The damage is done, and blaming cannot undo it. But the real damaging result of blaming is not its uselessness, it's what it does to our self esteem. You'd think blaming others or circumstances would make us feel better. But in actuality, it's just the opposite. Blaming forfeits our accountability. It surrenders too much power to other people.

Unfortunately, our society doesn't hold people as accountable for their actions as it should. Guilty by reason of insanity should not be a common, acceptable defense plea. That plea does more harm to the defendant than good. It reinforces the theory that blaming someone or something, such as insanity, is better than accepting responsibility. But it never is. It may keep someone out

66 The essential
conditions of everything
you do must be choice, love,
and passion. **99**

NADIA BOULANGER

of jail physically, but emotionally, that person stays incarcerated forever.

Turn on any morning or afternoon talk show. You'll hear people who blame the media, the government, their parents, their children, society, the list goes on and on. They haven't yet learned that blaming will keep them in bondage and prevent them from getting on with their lives. Learn from the past, then move on. We must accept the fact that no one has more control over our lives than we allow them to have. No one can make us feel anything without our permission. After all, aren't our emotions exclusively our own?

Dr. Wayne Dyer explains it this way: "If you take an orange and cut it in half, and squeeze one half, what comes out? The answer of course is juice. Why? Because that is what is inside." Elementary, right? Well, if you take a situation from our life where someone has pressured or squeezed us, what came out? Was it anger, hostility, depression? Why? Could it be because that was what was inside us at that time? It couldn't come out if it wasn't there. Work on what's inside of you and you'll be amazed how little you blame others. Most of us find more fault with others when we should be looking in the mirror.

Blaming stunts our growth. Here's a phrase that has helped me learn to stop blaming. "All people alive, at every moment of their life, did the best they could, or the only thing they could have done, given their knowledge and state of mind at that time." If we accept that truth that all of us did our best and all we could, given where our heads were at the time, it renders blame useless. Assigning things as right or wrong is wasting time and energy. The deed is done. Accept the things that happen to you, learn from them, and move on. That's all you can do.

SELF ESTEEM ZAPPER #2
GUILT AND REGRET

Guilt and regret are two more after-the-fact emotions. Just as with blame, the damage has already been done. Guilt and regret are a disease run rampant. I believe they kill more people than any other disease—maybe not kill their bodies, although some doctors attribute stress to guilt and regret, but they definitely kill the spirit. Both guilt and regret hold us back from achieving the things we want. They are silent deterrents. They are handicaps. The sooner we realize that guilt and regret can't change things, the sooner we can get on with the rest of our lives.

W Mitchell, a fellow speaker, has built a career proclaiming the message, "It's not what happens to you that is important, it's what you do about it."

There really is no such thing as good circumstances or bad circumstances. There are only circumstances. Things that happen to us are neutral. They become good or bad by what we do, or fail to do, with them. Everything that has happened has happened for a reason. A positive reason. Sometimes it takes a while to materialize, or for us to see the positive. I like the saying, "God never shuts a door without opening a window." The power in life is finding the windows.

SELF ESTEEM ZAPPER #3
COMPARISON

Comparison is not an-after-the-fact emotion, but it is useless nonetheless. Comparing is a no-win proposition. It's the deadly process of trying to always keep up with the Joneses. Comparing

66 **K**eep walking,
and
keep smiling. **99**

TINY TIM

leads to jealousy, and jealousy leads to feelings of inadequacy, which in turn, kill self esteem.

Living your life comparing yourself and your accomplishments to others also feeds blame, guilt, and regret. It's one big, vicious cycle. We have to learn to feel good about what we have and who we are, with no if's, and's or but's.

The mere fact that we compare ourselves to others shows that we have a self esteem problem. Comparing never cures low self esteem, even though sometimes we may come out ahead in the comparison. When we compare and win, we feel good about ourselves through another person's shortcomings. This creates only a false short-lived high that we often end up feeling guilty about or regretting later. It only masks the real problem, which is low self esteem. Accepting and liking yourself, the way you are, is an important ingredient in being able to sustain motivation.

When you live by the standards of others, you may be living a lie. You are living by self image, not by self esteem. We should not allow others to set our values for us. The only standards that are important are the ones we set for ourselves.

Don't be too hard on yourself. Just being you is already an incredible feat. There are over five billion people in the world, but only one you. No two people are exactly alike, and nobody is perfect. So comparing is useless. Here's a simple question to test your self esteem. If you can think of someone else you would rather be, you suffer from low self esteem.

Whenever I feel like a failure, I watch the movie *It's a Wonderful Life*. It is the perfect cure for feeling inadequate. In that movie, Jimmy Stewart was on the brink of committing suicide when an angel showed him what life would have been like without him. He realized he had touched literally hundreds of lives for the better without ever knowing it. The same is true for you. Becoming someone else would change history. Like yourself for who you are . . . you. You're one of a kind. So stop comparing.

Blame, guilt, and comparison don't lower esteem overnight; they slowly erode it over many years. But it doesn't have to take years to rebuild your self esteem. Here are three things we can begin to do immediately to help build it up.

SELF ESTEEM BUILDER #1
LEARNING

Knowledge and motivation go hand in hand. The more knowledgeable people are, the more naturally motivated they are. One of the more common causes of job burnout is having reached the end of the learning ladder. Not promotional ladder, learning ladder. Our minds need to stay challenged to stay sharp. Recent studies have linked energy to mind stimulation. Similar studies have linked mind stimulation from birth to age three to higher IQ's.

Learning is without a doubt one of the fastest ways to build up your self esteem. The average U.S. worker reads only two books pertaining to his or her occupation in their entire career. Sad, but true. Things are changing so fast in the '90s that many companies are beginning to realize that the rate at which employees learn is a primary factor in gaining competitive advantage. I believe the 1990s will go down in history as the decade that training and education really came to the forefront.

Learning is not limited to formal education, and learning should certainly not be the sole responsibility of employers. Learning should be a part of our everyday life. Take a nature

"*I didn't think motivation was part of the job.*"

walk, visit a museum, ask questions of others to learn from their experiences, or read a book that can expand your horizons. I've often said I can tell a lot about a person by the book, or lack of a book, on their nightstand. Make it a goal to learn something new every day. It will increase your knowledge, and your motivation.

SELF ESTEEM BUILDER #2
COMPLIMENTING

Complimenting others and using encouraging words is another way to build up self esteem. The premise is simple. We tend to compliment and encourage others more often when we feel good about ourselves, and we feel good about ourselves when we compliment and encourage others. It's the classic chicken or the egg routine, only it doesn't matter which comes first; they feed off each other.

I don't mean you should make up nice things to say; that would be nothing more than cheap flattery. But when you sincerely think something nice about someone else, say it. It can't work it's magic if we keep it inside. Our words have a significant impact on others. Many times we forget people's actions, but their words we remember. Words can burn a permanent impression on our subconscious. It is absolutely not true that "sticks and stones may break your bones, but words will never hurt you." Words hurt more. Words may not break bones, but they can break hearts. Our words should be builder uppers, not tearer downers.

But just as important as the impact our words have on others is the impact our words have on ourselves. Complimenting and encouraging others help to build up our own self esteem, and

66 Quit now,
you'll never make it.
If you disregard
this advice, you'll be
halfway there. **99**

DAVID ZUCKER

higher self esteem translates into higher levels of motivation. I don't know if this can be explained scientifically, but it can be explained emotionally. It is kin to the belief that it feels better to give than to receive.

Think of self esteem as a bank account. Giving to others makes a deposit in our emotional bank account. Blaming, criticizing, and the other esteem zappers act as withdrawals. The greater the balance, the higher your self esteem. The good news is that this is one account to which you can make many deposits every day. Build up your self esteem account, and more motivation will be your interest.

SELF ESTEEM BUILDER #3
BEING THANKFUL

Being thankful works much the same way as complimenting and encouraging others: it's an inner feel-good. But it isn't good enough just to be thankful, we have to verbalize it to build self esteem. If we're not thankful, we're sorrowful. We either feel good about what we have, or we feel angry or depressed about what we have.

Wanting more in life is good, it's what this book on motivation is all about. But wanting more because you believe that will bring you success and happiness is just a set-up for failure. One of the great misconceptions is that material things can make us happy. The truth is happiness does not come from outside of us, it comes from within. Believing happiness comes from external sources will rob us of esteem, and natural motivation. If you are not thankful for the little things, you won't be thankful for the bigger things. Get in the habit now. Don't wait to be thankful.

We tend to only take notice of the things we don't have, and ignore and take for granted the things we do have.

Like the other self esteem zappers, depression, pity, and sorrow make withdrawals on our esteem bank account. Thankfulness makes a deposit. Stop and proclaim the things you're thankful for. You'll be amazed at just how much there is, and how good you'll feel!

It's a Self Project

These are by no means the only things that zap and build self esteem. There are literally hundreds of contributors. But these are a few of the biggies. To increase your motivation, you'll need to increase your self esteem. Low self esteem is indeed a zapper, but you have final say over that. That's why they call it *self* esteem. It's a do-it-yourself project. You're in charge. It can't zap your motivation unless you allow it to do so. High self esteem is essential to your motivation foundation. Remember: It's a bank account, contribute to it every day and watch your personal power grow.

CHAPTER

Dreams

FIVE

The third builder and/or zapper is *dreams*. Dreams give us our direction, which is the foundation for sustained motivation. Anyone can and will have periodic bursts of motivation, but without a clear direction in life, motivation cannot be sustained. Dreams are the fuel for everyday motivation. Dreams are the ability to see the future in one's mind. This vision is the starting point. It is often said that lack of money does not make us poor, but lack of dreams does. Everything in life, both tangible and intangible begins with a dream.

Let me illustrate. You would agree that there was a time when this book did not exist in physical form, correct? Of course. How about the chair you're sitting on? Wasn't there a time when it did not exist physically? Certainly. Here's my point: Before these tangible things existed in physical form, they existed where? In someone's mind! Someone had the idea. They began as thoughts, visions. Someone had the dream. The dream gave birth to action and the rest is history.

Like motivation, dreams are hard to maintain. *Dreams are very fragile things:* they need to be guarded and nurtured. Many of us start out with dreams, only to allow them to die, or worse yet, let others kill them. Without dreams and direction, motivation becomes a chore. Dreams can build motivation, but they need constant nurturing. Just as flowers and plants need soil, sunlight and water to grow, dreams need three things to grow as well. They need alignment, optimism, and passion.

Alignment

Alignment is to dreams what soil is to plants. Dreams are embedded in our subconscious. They begin emotionally, and become logical. Yet for many people, dreams die because the emotional roots are not strong enough. One cause for this is that they are not aligned. Our dreams must be aligned and consistent with our internal value and belief system to grow stronger.

Inconsistent values act as an unseen force against motivation. It's like the ocean undercurrent. You can't see it, but before you know it, it can pull you under. Inconsistent values and beliefs work much the same way. If they are not properly aligned and consistent with what you're trying to achieve, they will ultimately sabotage your efforts. Our value and belief system is the body's infrastructure. They are the governing force behind all of our decisions and actions. If our dreams are not aligned and consistent with our values and beliefs, they become highly susceptible to the criticism and scrutiny of others.

An example of this is the person who is living someone else's dream. Perhaps a parent, spouse, boss, or friend. It may be the man who is struggling with his own business because he thought it was the right thing to do, but who has trouble getting out of bed in the morning. Or the opposite, a person who works for someone else who yearns for a business of her own. The mother who secretly wants an out-of-the-home career, or one who has a career and feels guilty because they are not at home with their children. The examples are many. In all of these cases motivation is a constant battle because of lack of alignment. You need to be true to the person in the mirror.

There is the well-known case of a salesperson who was given a very lucrative territory, one that had a six-figure potential. Yet despite the opportunity, she made only twenty-five thousand dollars. The next year, management demoted her to a territory where her predecessor made only fifteen thousand. It was a ter-

66 **O**ur aspirations

are our

possibilities. **99**

ROBERT BROWNING

rible territory by all accounts. To everyone's surprise, she broke all records by making twenty-five thousand dollars. Believing she was now ready for the bigger territory, management moved her back into a lucrative territory where she continued to earn just twenty-five thousand dollars. Through counseling, the truth came out. Her husband made twenty-five thousand dollars per year. As did her father, and all of her friends. She saw herself as a twenty-five-thousand-dollar-per-year person. Her efforts were sabotaged by her own internal value and belief system.

This example is not as uncommon as you might think. Give yourself the following alignment quiz to see if you might discover any inconsistencies.

1. Are you really happy with your life?
2. Do you like what you do?
3. Do you take pride in your work? Or is it just a job?
4. What would you do if money were not an issue?
5. What hobbies do you have? Favorite activities?
6. Where do you see yourself in five years? Ten years? Twenty years?
7. What things do you do better than anyone else?
8. What were your childhood dreams?
9. What is your definition of success?
10. What are you passionate about?

I hope you took time to ponder those questions. Dreams can be a powerful builder of motivation, but only if they are aligned and consistent with our beliefs. Otherwise, you may be spinning your wheels and going nowhere.

Optimism

Optimism is a deep-rooted belief that things always work out for the better. It is realizing that the past does not equal the future. The irony of optimism is that those statements are not just examples of optimism. They are absolute truths! The fact that some people do not believe them reduces them to just credos for optimists. But just because some do not believe their truth does not make them any less true. Optimism is truly believing the past does not equal the future.

Those who believe the future will be worse than the past are called pessimists. This lack of hope is not only harmful to motivation, but to overall health as well. A recent study by a psychologist at the University of Pittsburgh reports that a pessimistic outlook actually shortens the lifespan of adults under sixty who suffer a recurrence of cancer. Similar studies have shown pessimism can even impair our immune function. Pessimism is, without a doubt, an illness that greatly influences our ability to stay motivated.

Optimists, on the other hand, expect good things to happen, are natural dreamers, and are able to sustain motivation for longer periods of time. Optimists realize that emotions are not caused by events, but rather by thoughts. The law of expectations says that what we expect to happen, usually happens. You can not control most events, but you do have direct control over your thoughts. Maintaining this power is the basis for being and staying optimistic.

A pessimist's emotions are victims to events.

When something bad happens to you, learn to ask yourself, "Will this affect my life five years from now?" If the answer is no, forget it. Optimists don't allow events to alter their emotions. Do not dwell on the problems; rather focus on solutions. This is not to say that optimists try to ignore or mask problems. Quite the opposite. They confront problems head on. Confronting problems is looking for solutions. Complaining or feeling bad or sorry for yourself makes the problem worse. Keep your eyes on your dream. By doing this, you will not only stay optimistic, but your motivation levels will stay high as well.

Passion

Passion is the fire inside. Alignment can show you what and where your dreams are. Optimism can show you how to keep dreams alive, but passion is the why! Victor Frankyl, a World War II survivor of Auschwitz, once wrote, "If you have a strong enough *why*, you will figure out the how." Passion is to dreams what octane is to gasoline. Passion will keep you going when logic tells you to give up.

It's a good thing Thomas Edison had passion. He was told by a grade school teacher that he was too stupid to learn anything. A newspaper editor in Kansas City fired Walt Disney, claiming he didn't have any good ideas. Beethoven's music teacher called him hopeless as a composer. Several magazine editors once refused to print any of Emily Dickinson's poems because they didn't rhyme. Leo Tolstoy flunked out of college.

If you have a strong enough why, the how's take care of themselves. Passion keeps you going and overcomes many obstacles. Here's a rule to live by: Whatever you get passionate about will get passionate about you. But only if you get passionate and excited first. If you want to have an exciting career, you'll first need to get excited about it. If you want an exciting marriage, get ex-

66 I always wanted
to be somebody, but I
should have been
more specific. **99**

LILY TOMLIN

cited about your marriage. If you want to make a lot of money, get excited about making money. Getting excited is always the first step. Remember when you were little. Did you wait until the morning of your birthday to get excited, or were you excited weeks, maybe months in advance? Probably the latter. And when we look back to our childhood memories, it is that excitement and anticipation that we remember most vividly.

Keep in mind that passion can be built. Sometimes passion is automatic and involuntary, but other times it must be built. Passion is built by taking many small steps in the direction of your dreams. Once your dream is identified, and you're sure it is aligned with your values and beliefs, take a small step toward it.

I once had a woman in one of my seminars whose dream was to own her own bed and breakfast inn. I asked her what she was doing to move closer to owning one. She said, "Nothing right now. I can't afford to buy one now." It was obvious her passion needed to be built back up. I advised her to start small, and gave her the assignment of interviewing at least three bed and breakfast owners in the next month. Just call them up and talk to them. She said, "That seems easy enough." Well, to make a long story short, over the next three months she talked to dozens of inn owners from all over the country, and met personally with six of them. After six months, she was a member of the National Association for Bed and Breakfast Inns, and was working part time at one of them. Over the next few months I didn't hear much from her. Then one year, almost to the day of my seminar, she called to report that she had just made an offer to buy her own inn. Although she credits me for her success, it was really her passion for her dream that made it come true. I merely gave her a push. Passion is vital to keeping your dreams alive, and keeping your dreams alive is vital to staying motivated. I recently saw a bumper sticker I liked: "Passion—get it or else!" Enough said.

Dreams sometimes come and go. Some just take a sabbatical, and get reborn. Others get replaced by new dreams. Some dreams take years to come true; some never come true. But it's the <u>hope</u> that's important to motivation. Lack of hope and dreams chisel away at your motivation foundation. Never let your dreams die or, worse yet, let others kill them. It's a miracle that dreams can be so fragile, yet so powerful. Hold on to your dreams and motivation will hold on to you!

66 The great thing
in this world is not
so much where we are,
but in what direction
we are moving. **99**

OLIVER WENDELL HOLMES

CHAPTER

Discipline

SIX

The final "builder and/or zapper" is, as you might have guessed, *Discipline*. This one is simple. Having discipline is a builder. Lack of discipline is a zapper. Discipline is the ability to stick to your plans even when you may not feel like it. Without positive discipline, motivation is handicapped, since motivation feeds off progress. People with positive discipline have not only a solid work ethic, but a proper balance in all phases of their life. This leads to ultimate control over one's destiny. Lack of discipline, on the other hand, is often characterized by an inability to commit, breaking one's word, or most commonly, procrastination. All three are negative manifestations of lack of discipline and are habit forming. Let's examine them and the ways to make discipline work for us instead of against us.

Procrastination

Procrastination is discipline delayed. It is a time problem, which is almost always coupled with one or two other motivation zappers. Procrastination is deadly to motivation.

This truth was recognized over two hundred years ago by Ben Franklin when he said, "Never put off to tomorrow what could be done today." This has a dual meaning. The first, obvious meaning is that not putting things off will make us more productive in our daily lives. The second meaning is that being productive today will make us more motivated to be productive tomorrow. Remember, we've already discussed in Chapter Two that motivation feeds off momentum and action. The opposite of momentum is procrastination.

I call procrastination a time problem because people who procrastinate usually believe that time is against them. "Not

66 Laziness is
nothing more than
the habit of resting before
you get tired. **99**

JULES RENARD

enough time, so why bother?" kind of thing. For these people procrastination is coupled with a limiting belief as well. This limiting belief can cause frustration, lowered self esteem, and perhaps even an alignment problem. The truth about time is that we all have the same amount. There's just twenty-four hours in a day, seven days in a week, and three hundred sixty-five days per year for every one of us. It's what we do with it that matters. How is it that some people accomplish many great feats day, week, and year after year, while some people can only manage to do just enough to barely survive? The answer is discipline.

Here are a few simple ideas to overcome procrastination, and build positive discipline.

1. TAKE ACTION—Action cures a hesitation problem. No matter how small the action may be, do something. Start by making "to do" lists. This is the quickest and easiest way to discipline yourself. Make a list each night before bed of the things you'd like to accomplish the next day. As you do each one, check it off.

This simple exercise does many things toward building motivation. First, it creates momentum. You'll be amazed at how much more you'll feel like doing when your plan is written down. Second, it will build self esteem. Nothing beats the feeling of accomplishment. Third, those daily "lists" will help build and keep you on the track of your dreams. Reward yourself with something small for every day you achieve everything that is on your list. There will be days when you won't be able to do everything. That's ok. Learn from it. What part of your day could you have altered? Or did you just try to bite off more than you could chew?

Never, however, go to sleep with items still on that day's list. Even if you didn't do them, cross them off and add them to the next day's list. You don't get a reward, but at least you're starting fresh again the next day. There is nothing worse than lying in bed lamenting over unaccomplished tasks.

2. BE HERE NOW—It's ok to plan and dream for the future, but live in the "now" at all times. Whatever you're doing, and wherever you are, BE THERE. You lower your effectiveness for whatever you're doing when your mind is someplace else. Who has not missed an exit while driving because their minds were elsewhere? It's wonderful to day dream, but only when that's what you set out to do. Day dreaming, or mind wandering as I like to call it, not only causes you to take longer at what you are doing, but drastically increases the probability for mistakes. Do it right the first time. Discipline your mind to stay with and complete the task at hand before moving on.

As with making lists, this does several things toward building motivation. One, it makes you more effective, thus creating momentum. Second, by cutting down on mistakes and second tries, you'll feel better about yourself. That's higher self esteem. Third, it builds a winning work ethic by training your mind to be able to focus on one thing at a time. This ability to focus is what allows people to break through many boards with a single karate chop. I even believe one's mind has the capacity to move objects, simply by concentrating on them. This phenomenon is called telekinesis, and it's not just science fiction. We just haven't quite discovered how to tap into yet. But we will.

"But Honey, if you want me to be motivated,
I need my rest."

Breaking Your Word

Discipline means little if we cannot keep our word. I don't want to turn this into a first grade lesson, but what do we have if we don't have our word? Too often we nonchalantly toss around promises with little intent of following through. Remember from Chapter Three, what we say is what we get. If we get in the habit of saying falsehoods, our subconscious mind goes along. Next thing you know, we're cynical and untrusting of others.

But this goes beyond lying. The real damage is not what it does to others, but what it does to ourselves. Most lies are not verbal. Most are nonverbal. However, they are only nonverbal in sound. To our subconscious, they are every bit as verbal. When we lie to ourselves our inner consciousness goes into battle. It's the classic good versus evil scenario, only internal. This battle obviously lowers self esteem and often leads to guilt, and it is also tremendously mentally draining, because this silent, inner conflict lowers the body's natural supply of adrenaline. It stands to reason, lowered energy levels lead to lowered productivity.

Inability to Commit

So, you don't want to procrastinate, or break your word, so why not just avoid all commitments completely? People who lack positive discipline find it difficult to make even the slightest commitment. And vice versa. I saved this motivation builder for last. The reason is obvious. Unless you are committed to building a solid motivation foundation, all else is futile. Think of commitment as discipline glue. Good old fashioned schoolroom glue. Commitments create positive discipline and act as the glue that

66 In the last analysis, the only freedom is the freedom to discipline ourselves. **99**

BERNARD BARUCH

holds motivation together. Our commitments make us unique. The way we respond to our commitments can be a factor in staying motivated. The key is making the commitment and then accepting responsibility to see it through.

My first real, full-time job was a selling position. I was excited because I knew I had what it takes to be a successful salesperson. I even relocated to begin my new career. I had plenty of motivation, but what I didn't have was commitment. I thought commitments were just for relationships. I would get sidetracked easily. My work ethic soon began to take a nose dive.

No one ever told me that selling was such hard work. I was motivated when it was easy, but frustrated when it became difficult. Because I did not have commitment, I lacked the positive discipline to carry me through the times when my excitement waned. I did what a lot of us do when we fail, I blamed anything and everything I could. I was fired! Needless to say, I was zapped! I was negative, my self esteem suffered, I questioned my dream of being a salesperson, and discipline was all but nonexistent.

Commitments hold it together. Being committed to the dream without being committed to the discipline necessary to make it happen is a set-up for failure. I picked myself up, brushed myself off and went on. The true sign of a winner is not how many times you fall, but how many times you get up. Having learned from my experience of not committing, I went on to set many sales records in my next position.

A plan without commitment is like trying to hit a baseball without a bat. You might have heard the story of Cortez, the Spanish explorer who founded Mexico. When his ships landed at what is now Mexico he sent his troops out to survey the situation. They came back pleading to turn back, saying the natives outnumbered them at least four to one. Cortez thought for a moment, then ordered his troops to burn their ships. His troops, fearing Cortez almost as much as they did the natives, did as they were told. The rest is history. They went on to claim Mexico. By burning their ships, they eliminated all options. They had to commit. There was no contingency plan. Whenever you have a plan A, and a plan B, you dilute your chances of succeeding with plan A. Committing means burning your ships. Think what that would do for your motivation!

Take a Habit Inventory

We're all creatures of habit. Habits are powerful things. So the first step in beginning to develop positive discipline is to take inventory of your current habits. Discipline is made up of hundreds of individual habits. Many are productive, many are counter-productive. You'll need to find out which are which.

Make a list of what you believe are your good habits and your bad habits. Don't try to rationalize your bad habits. Use the question, "Is it moving me closer or farther from my dreams?" The ones that move you closer are good habits; the others will need to be changed.

As we discussed briefly in Chapter Two, the best way to change a habit is to replace it. Remember it only takes twenty-one days in a row to create a new habit. Twenty-one days, that's it! But like anything worthwhile, it will take positive discipline. Today is day one. You can do it. The past does not equal the future. Don't try to change all your bad habits at once. Take twenty-one days for each one. You'll see that they get easier as

66 Everything I did
in my life that was worthwhile
I caught hell for. **99**

EARL WARREN

you go. The hardest one is always the first one. Stick to it. Be committed, do not give up when the going gets tough. The act of giving up is diametrically opposed to motivation.

Winston Churchill eloquently summed this up one day as he took the microphone to give a commencement address, "Never, never, never, never, never, never, give up!" Then he sat down. When quitting is no longer an option, that's the beginning of discipline, and lasting motivation.

66 **J**ust do it. 99

NIKE

PART

3

THE
SUSTAINERS

CHAPTER

Cues

SEVEN

66 Throughout history, the most common debilitating human ailment has been cold feet. 99

ANONYMOUS

By this point you should understand the importance of having a solid motivation foundation. Please understand that there are many other factors that will affect motivation. But if your foundation is strong, you will be equipped to weather any temporary set-back. Also by now, you realize that merely wanting something is not necessarily enough to cause you to take action. By not taking action, or delaying action, you will eventually diminish your desire for that particular something. Just as motivation needs a foundation, it also needs to be sustained. In the next three chapters, you will learn three techniques to get and sustain motivation. Naturally I call these techniques *motivation sustainers*. These sustainers are the basis for somapsychotics, which I introduced in Chapter Two. Somapsychotics is the programming of the mind through physical, rather than mental means. Remember, matter over mind.

The following sustainers are ways to achieve somapsychotics. The first is the use of *cues*. Cues are external reminders for positive thinkmodes. Cues are centered around the theory that whatever we continually hold in our conscious mind will be acted on by our subconscious mind. Cues are external stimuli that instruct, inspire, or remind us of our intentions, thus holding the thoughts in our conscious mind. Let's explore how the use of cues can help us in our daily quest to get and stay motivated.

What are Cues?

Signs, signs, everywhere signs. These words from a famous song could well have been, "Cues, cues, everywhere cues." Cues should not be new to any of us. We grew up with cues. They're all around us. Cues get their name from the entertainment industry, which invented the use of "cue cards" to remind actors of their lines. The dictionary defines cues as a reminder or prompting to do something. Cues tell us or remind us what to do. For example, road signs direct us when to stop, go, take caution, yield, etc. Billboards spark us to buy certain products. "No smoking" signs tell us when smoking is not allowed. A clock signals the time of day. A danger sign warns us of trouble ahead.

Cues are not limited to visual stimuli. The sounding of the dinner bell has for centuries proclaimed that dinner is ready. The bugle and the alarm clock signal the dawn of a new day. The "Star Spangled Banner" reminds us that there's no place like home. There are cues for all of the five senses.

Remember when your mother told you to tie a string around your finger when she wanted you to remember something? Cues can act as that proverbial string around your finger. They are mental reminders that stimulate an action, feeling, or thought.

Up until now, we've been living and responding to cues that were set up and placed by others. This is one of the reasons why our motivation fluctuates. Our personal motivation is reactionary to cues that are not our own. Why not stack the deck? By using cues, you can create your own personal road signs. You can create the reminders or directions that have special meaning to you. Your cues can be banners, signs, posters, pictures, quotes, bells, whistles, just about anything at all.

Why Use Cues?

Cues remind us of actions, feelings, or thoughts that we want to adopt in our lives. There isn't a goal-setting program in the world that doesn't advocate putting pictures of your goals on your re-

66 The hero,
therefore, is the person
who has been able to battle past
their personal and historical
limitations. **99**

JOSEPH CAMPBELL

frigerator, mirror, etc. The use of cues in goal setting can dramatically increase the likelihood of attaining your goals. The reason is quite simple. By continually registering your intents in your conscious mind, they begin to filtrate into your subconscious mind.

We've already established your subconscious mind never rests. It constantly is working to take action on the things it is given. Remember the movie "War Games"? The giant computer called "WOPR" kept trying combination after combination until it found the correct one to achieve its mission. Your subconscious mind works exactly the same way. What you program it to go after, it faithfully tackles until completion, or reprogramming. Cues program your subconscious through conscious stimuli.

How to Set Up Your Cues

The purpose, form, content, and placement of cues are paramount to their effectiveness. First decide on what you want your cues to accomplish. What is the purpose? What do you want your cues to remind you of or direct you to do? Decide on the end result you'd like to achieve. Then decide on the physical form of your cue. Cues may be pictures or photos of your goals and dreams. Cues may be motivational sayings or quotes. Or they can be instructional, like a cue that might be near your telephone that simply says, SMILE! Customer service departments all over the world use that one.

Once you've decided on the purpose and form of your cue, then decide on what you want it to say. Choose your content carefully. You'll want to make sure whatever words or images you select are able to clearly and concisely project your purpose. The words or images of your cues should be inspirational to you. They should get you thinking about the results you're using the cue to achieve. They should get you to take action.

Once you have identified the purpose, form, and content of your cues, you'll need to select their locations. Placement of cues is critical to their success. Cues should be placed in conspicuous locations and where you need their help the most. If you're trying to lose weight, place a cue near, on, or in your refrigerator. Cues on your nightstand ensure that their message is among the last inputs of the day. Perhaps you can place one on your bathroom mirror to begin the day on the right foot. Cues can be on your desk at work, or in your car. Wherever you need them, cues can be there. Associations and corporations place banners in well-traveled places to support their theme and inspire the attendees. Cues are everywhere. After a while, they become like a good friend, always there to support you and lift you up.

An Example of Proper Cuing

At one point in my life I suffered from a very common ailment that I call "snooze alarmitis." This ailment is characterized by chronically and habitually delaying the start of the day by engaging the snooze button. For years this habit haunted me. I knew that by beginning the day sluggishly, it set the tone for the entire day. I knew that instead of feeling remorse at the sound of my alarm clock, I should be thankful for the opportunity of a new day and greet it with proper enthusiasm. But just wanting that to happen was not enough to make it so. Upon awakening I would still only see and hear the alarm clock.

"I hate that thing!"

I had to create a cue that would get me up and going quicker. Since I am a motivational-saying junkie, I decided on the perfect quote to use as my cue. "The Goddess of Athena will lift you up, but you have to raise your hand." This saying is a cross between "God helps those who help themselves" and "the difference between ordinary and extraordinary is just a little extra."

To make sure this was the first thing I would see when I opened my eyes, I placed it on the wall facing my bed. I also taped it around my alarm clock so that I literally had to read it to shut the alarm off.

Since I hadn't yet formed my new habit, I couldn't just jump out of bed. I got up rather slowly at first. But soon the habit of getting up when the alarm sounded took over. Now it feels out of place for me to hit the snooze button. The use of cues helped me replace a negative habit with a positive one. I was sold. Cues are scattered throughout my house in strategic places. As I'm sure you've noticed by now, my favorite motivational sayings command their own pages of this book. Feel free to borrow them for your own use. They make great cues! After all, a book on motivation is not the same without great motivational sayings.

A Final Thought About Cues

Cues do not necessarily have to be tangible objects. Cues can be verbal as well. I am convinced that one of the reasons I am a sales trainer and speaker is due to the cues I received from my mother growing up. Beginning when I was three, my mother, noticing my gift of gab and persuasiveness, proclaimed that I would either be a salesperson or a preacher like Billy Graham when I grew up.

She would repeat her prophesy time and time again through the years. Her verbal cues must have sunk in. Today I am both a preacher and a salesperson. I travel the country preaching about selling. Do not underestimate the power of cues. Many existing circumstances originated as childhood cues—good or bad. As we read this, many circumstances in your future are being shaped by current cues. Here is your chance to create positive, empowering cues, ones that will get and keep you motivated.

66 All the wonders
you seek are
within yourself. **99**

SIR THOMAS BROWNE

CHAPTER

EIGHT

66 The secret
of happiness is not
doing what one likes,
but in liking what
one does. **99**

James Barrie

The second "motivation sustainer" is to build and use *links*. Links, sometimes called triggers or anchors, are the internal subconscious version of cues. Links are a sensory stimulus that is connected to a specific emotion. For example, do you ever hear a song on the radio that automatically triggers your memory of a particular feeling? It might be good or bad, but that song is linked to a specific experience. This is classic psychological association. Getting goosebumps when you see an American flag, smiling when you smell Grandma's apple pie, or feeling your heart beat faster when you hear a creaky door are all examples of links. Links can be made through any of the five senses: sounds, images, tastes, touches, and smells.

Links are created every day, and most of the time without our ever knowing about it. These are called "unconditioned links." A good example of an unconditioned link happened years ago when my sister and I were young children. One night after a dinner of pork chops and rice, my sister became ill. The illness, we would find out later, had absolutely nothing to do with the meal; however, subconsciously she linked the rice to getting sick. From then on she would not eat rice. To this day she does not have any recall of why she doesn't like rice, but the mere thought of it triggers ill feelings inside. A link was created without her knowledge.

This is not uncommon. Links are created daily. Are there ever times when you experience an emotion without knowing why? Sometimes, for seemingly no reason at all, I feel depressed. Conversely, there are times I can't rationally explain my exuberant mood. I now realize these are results of unconditioned links.

It is my intention to make you aware of the links you might be creating and how to consciously create links that can help you stay motivated. Most people do not realize that they hold the power to create their own system of links. Links we create consciously are called "conditioned links."

A classic example of conditioned links would be the experiments of Pavlov. Pavlov tested his theory of response conditioning by ringing a dinner bell just before feeding his dogs. The sight and smell of the impending dinner would cause the dogs to salivate. But after a few days he noticed that he could just ring the bell, without producing any food, and this would cause the dogs to salivate. He had created a link in the dogs' minds between the sound of the dinner bell and a physiological response, salivation.

To really see the use of conditioned links in action, all you need to do is watch television. Commercials are geared to create links. Beer makers use pretty girls in bikinis and muscular men, sneaker makers use athletes, cereal makers use cartoon characters, and so on. They are attempting to link the feelings and popularity of the image with the product. The message is that you'll attract more members of the opposite sex if you drink Brand X beer, if you wear Brand X sneaker you'll be like Mike, and if you eat Brand X cereal, you can eat what the Power Rangers eat.

Let's look at how you can create your own links to help you get and stay motivated, and to make sure you are not creating negative links that will accidently handicap your motivation. There are three steps to creating a motivation link.

STEP #1

RECALL THE EMOTION

Let me start by saying you already know how to get motivated. If you've ever been motivated in the past, even just once, you know how. Creating a link will simply allow you to tap into that feeling whenever you want. The first step is to find a quiet place where you can totally relax. Sit upright in a chair so you're comfortable, but don't run the risk of falling asleep. Close your eyes. Allow your mind to wander for a minute or two. Then recall a time when you were really motivated. If you've never been motivated in the past, it is impossible to create a link. But if you have, and of course you have, your subconscious mind will remember how to do it. If you've done it before, you can do it again.

Give your subconscious a little help. It is essential that you recall the emotion in vivid detail. Visualize yourself at a time when you were motivated. I mean really motivated. Not just a little motivated. The greater the detail in which you visualize, the stronger the link will be. If you need help visualizing, ask yourself these questions. What were you doing? What were you picturing in your mind? How did you move your body? What expression did you have on your face? What did you say? What did you say to yourself? Relive the experience in your mind. Continue this recall until you are absolutely at the peak of the emotion, until you are experiencing the same intensity of motivation as in the time you are recalling. When you're brimming with feelings of motivation then you are ready to create the link.

STEP #2

CREATE THE LINK

Once you have reached the peak emotionally, create the link with a specific, unique physical stimulus. While continuing to visualize, pat the top of your head, pinch your knee, click your heels together, pump your fists, do anything that is unique. Remember what you do and exactly how you do it. This action will get etched in your subconscious mind. You'll need to repeat the stimulus exactly as it was created to make an effective link. It is important, however, that the stimulus you choose be out of the ordinary. If the stimulus action you select is too familiar, it will dilute the future effectiveness of the link. For example, if you normally scratch your nose a lot, choose something else.

Continue to visualize yourself as completely motivated while providing the stimulus. Repeat this stimulus a few times to ensure that the link has been created. It is better to err on the side of to much than not enough. A few times, however, should be sufficient to create your motivation link.

STEP #3
NEUTRALIZE

After creating the link, you must come down from the emotional high in order for your body to process what has just happened. Neutralize yourself by changing your physiology. Get up, stretch, and think of something new. This should help to zap you out of the intense state you were in when you created your link.

It is now time to test the link to see if it took. You should be able to instantly experience the feelings of motivation by simply using your link. Whenever and wherever you need to be motivated, your link is the answer. Unless . . .

Troubleshooting Your Link

If your link does not work, don't get discouraged. It can only be for one of five reasons.

66 The worst
bankrupt in the world is the
person who has lost their
enthusiasm. **99**

H. W. ARNOLD

First, the intensity of your recall may not have been strong enough. If the experience you chose to use as your motivation recall is not powerful enough, choose another experience. It is vital that you choose to recall a time when you were extremely, no-holds-barred motivated. It is not enough to choose a time when you were somewhat motivated. You could have also chosen the right experience, but didn't recall it intensely or vividly enough.

The second explanation of a failed link is that you may not have been at the peak of the recall when you created it. Sometimes it can be hard to know when you're at the peak. Go with your instincts. If you still can't tell, link early and often to make sure you've hit the peak. You can't link too much, but you can not link enough.

Third, your stimulus may not have been unique or specific enough. Snapping your fingers would not make a good link because it is too familiar of an action. Do something unusual, something you would not do unless intentionally. The fourth possible error could be in the way you are repeating the stimulus. It has to be done the exact same way as when you created the link. Even the slightest difference will not cause your subconscious mind to make the connection. If your link was created by pinching your knee, you must pinch your knee the exact way in the exact same place for the link to work.

Lastly, it could be that something else happened while you created the link that you may not remember. If you inadvertently scratched your hand during the linking process, that stimulus became part of your link. Anything that happens—any movement, sound, touch, smell, etc.—while you're in that peak state will get linked to that state. This is why it is key to create your link in a quiet, neutral setting. For any of these reasons for link failure, the diagnosis is the same. Repeat the process.

Using Your Link for Specific Tasks

Now you know how to create a link to feel motivated. But how about motivating yourself to do a particular task? You can use the link you have already created to instantly become enthusiastic to do just about anything you want, regardless of how you may feel about that task. First go someplace quiet and decide on the task or project you want to be motivated for. Then visualize yourself doing that particular task. Visualize every little detail. Then when the image is at peak, create a link. Let's call this your task link. Next, neutralize. Rest for a minute. Visualization can be hard work.

Now it is time to fuse the two links together. Clear your mind, then engage both links at the same time. For example, pinch your knee while clicking your heels. This is called *dual linking*. The stronger of the two emotions always overtakes the other. Meaning: The positiveness of your motivation link must be stronger than the negativeness of your task link for this to work. For example, if you're creating an exercise task link, but your dislike for exercising is stronger than the recall you are using, the link will not work. If anything, you might have created a physical link for feeling distaste for exercising. But if your recall is stronger, the result should be a new-found motivation for the task itself, in this case, exercising. The recalled feelings of motivation replace the dislike of the task. It is like recording over an old cassette tape in your mind. To ensure the fusing, visualize yourself doing the task enthusiastically.

A Final Word on Links

I know you are probably skeptical about this whole link thing. I was too at first. Keep an open mind. It is possible, however, to expect too much from the links you create. They are not magic. Remember, the intensity of the link is only as powerful as the intensity of your recall. Don't expect an earth-shattering transformation. False expectations and skepticism can dilute the effectiveness of links. Links are for real. Many of the emotions we experience on a daily basis may be traced to links that have been created subconsciously. Now you can take control of what gets linked. I've shown you how to use links for motivation purposes, but many other uses exist. Continue your education on links. It will be worth your while. I promise.

66 The highest
reward for a person's toil
is not what they
get for it, but what they
become by it. **99**

JOHN RUSKIN

Endorphin Raising Activities (ERAs)

NINE

The last technique necessary to learn to help sustain motivation is to use our own bodies' greatest natural resource, *endorphins.* Endorphins are the end result of positive links. They are the driving force behind "somapsychotics." Motivation and endorphins are almost synonymous terms. As with motivation, endorphins are effects, not causes. They are not psychological. They are physiological.

Have you or anyone you've known ever used the phrase "high on life" to describe their exuberance? Have you ever been "pumped up" emotionally? Are there times when you want to run around giving everyone a "high five?" These are examples of the effects of endorphins. Endorphins are the psycho-neuro chemical our brain produces that triggers the flow of adrenaline. They are the body's natural morphine, or pain killer. In lay terms, they make us feel good.

Are Endorphins Good for Us?

I'll answer that with an emphatic YES! In an effort not to get too clinical, allow me to use a simple analogy. Think of yourself as your own pharmacist. You can *choose* HOW MUCH of this "wonder drug" you need, and WHEN you need it! Endorphins are never out of stock. They are always on call in your internal pharmacy. To continue the analogy, whenever you are experiencing motivation fluctuation, write yourself a prescription for endorphins. Go ahead. Get addicted. Unlike most synthetic drugs, endorphins are a positive addiction.

What prescription should you write? That depends on where you are, who you're with, and how strong a dose you need. You

66 **M**an's mind,
once stretched by a new idea,
never regains its original
dimensions. **99**

OLIVER WENDELL HOLMES

decide on the appropriate *endorphin raising activity*, ERA, that is required at that time. ERAs are causes; the desired feelings, increased endorphins and motivation, are the effects. No medical school training is necessary; just knowing which causes to use is sufficient. To help you, I'll give you some of the most effective ERAs.

ERA #1

EXERCISE

Have you ever wondered why you seem to have more energy after you exercise than you did before you started? The answer is an increased flow of endorphins. You may be sore, but you feel good inside. It's that feeling of pride and accomplishment that causes endorphins to be produced. Now you certainly didn't need me to tell you that exercise is important to the physical health of your body. But maybe you were not aware how important it is for your mental health as well. Doctors claim that exercise is the number one endorphin producing activity we can do. Even a small amount of exercise will increase endorphin levels. Now you have one more reason to exercise.

ERA #2

LAUGHTER

You've heard it said: laughter is the best medicine. Nothing reduces stress and produces endorphins faster than laughing. A noted physician at Harvard Medical School attempted to test the medicinal value of laughter. He gave each Harvard grad a questionnaire which he translated into what he called their "humor quotient" (HQ). Those grads with higher HQs went on not only to live healthier lives, but were worth more financially as well.

Many hospitals today practice laugh therapy. They have their patients stand in a row at set intervals and laugh. No jokes, no funny shows, no props. They have to make the laughing sound. The physiological response is the same in both real and faked laughter. Your mind does not know the difference. Endorphins are produced either way. It is interesting to note that almost all cases of sustained fake laughter eventually turn into genuine laughter. Remember somapsychotics. The art of laughing can change your thinking. Matter over mind.

Laughing raises the spirit, not to mention the spirits of those around you. Laughing is extremely contagious and highly influential. This is why many television comedies use canned laughter. We tend to laugh if we hear others laughing. Learn to laugh for no reason at all. Laugh just for the fun, and health, of it!

ERA #3
SMILING

There is something magical about a smile. Salespeople who greet the customer with a smile have a 15 percent greater chance of making a sale than those who do not smile. Waiters and waitresses who greet their tables with a smile earn on average 27 percent higher tips. Even Las Vegas has learned the power of a smile. Black Jack dealers in Las Vegas who smile while playing consistently bring in 5 percent more revenue than non-smiling dealers. The reason: people are more likely to play longer when they believe they are playing with the dealer as opposed to playing against the dealer. Now you know to avoid the smiling dealers.

66 The only time
you can't afford to fail
is the last
time you try. **99**

CHARLES KETTERING

Smiling not only benefits us externally, it benefits us internally as well. Dr. Dale Anderson, my fellow speaker and a physician, refers to a smile as "the costume of health." The actual physical formation of a smile produces endorphins, which, in turn, makes us healthier. At some of my seminars I demonstrate the internal magic of smiling. I bring someone to the front of the room and ask that person to give me a huge, wide-eyed grin. A real S.E.G., if you know what I mean. I have my subject stand up straight, on the balls of the feet. Then I ask him or her to try to feel depressed without losing the smile or changing physical posture. Very few can do it. It is virtually impossible for the body to feel depressed and smile at the same time. Smiling, like laughing, is also highly contagious. So if you'd like others to smile more at you, smile more at others. It can brighten their day, not to mention what it can do for you.

ERA #4
MUSIC

Charlie "Tremendous" Jones says music is the one thing that bypasses the brain and goes straight to the heart. Music is medicine to the soul. Music captures the heart, but thanks to endorphins, it doesn't totally bypass the brain. Sometimes when I get down, the only thing that works is music. We've already talked about music as a link, but music as an endorphin raiser is equally effective. It's a picker upper. I can still sing the words to my high school fight song. There are times when I get so down the only thing that helps is music. I've played my favorite song hundreds of times. Think of how many endorphins I must have produced!

ERA #5

PEP TALKS

There is a time, when I was in the sixth grade, that I'll never forget. I was an average athlete in a neighborhood of great athletes, so during annual basketball try-outs I was more than a bit nervous. Try-outs consisted of taking free throws and lay-ups in front of all the coaches in hopes of being drafted by one of them.

This particular year, much to my surprise, I was one of the first players chosen. I remember the coach pulling me aside and telling me that I had great potential and I would be the player which he would build the entire team around. I was "his rock!" I never forgot that little pep talk, even though half way through the season my family moved out of the area. It made me realize the impact that words have on others. To some extent, that was the day my dream of being a professional speaker was born.

Since then, pep talks became a regular part of my life. I looked for them. From friends, teachers, relatives, girlfriends, anyone who would oblige. I went to any seminar I could that would provide me with encouragement. I became a self-help junkie when others for some reason could not fulfill my pep talk requirements, I gave them to myself. Literally. I took countless long walks, by myself, engaged in rousing one-way communication. Some of those private pep talks became the basis for future speeches.

But it wasn't until many years later that I learned why those pep talks were so important. They were endorphin raising activities! I learned that my most productive times were right after a pep talk. It's no secret that most companies have their sales meetings on Monday mornings, or why the best time to make a sales call is right after a made sale. The answer, of course, is endorphins.

ERA #6
THE HUMAN TOUCH

The loving, supportive touch of someone who cares about us is another endorphin-raising activity. Hugs, holding hands, high fives, and back rubs, are just a few ways to produce endorphins. Even petting animals has been proven to raise endorphin levels. It is documented that senior citizens who own a dog have 16 percent fewer doctor visits than those who do not have dogs. Studies have even shown that the act of dog petting can be directly tied to better health. Food, water, and the human touch are necessary to sustain life not to mention motivation!

Anything Else?

These mentioned activities are by no means the only ones that produce endorphins. In fact, all the motivation builders we discussed in earlier chapters—a positive attitude, high self esteem, a passionate dream, and self discipline—also contribute to raising endorphin levels. Things like a bright sunny day, beautiful scenery, the sound of a loved one's voice, and even R.E.M. (rapid eye movement) sleep can also produce endorphins.

R.E.M. sleep is the period of very deep sleep the body requires to function at optimum levels. One of the reasons R.E.M. sleep is so rejuvenating is because of its high production of endorphins. No amount of non-R.E.M. sleep can take the place of R.E.M. sleep for this very reason.

Endorphins are indeed necessary ingredients to getting and staying motivated. I hope I've been able to provide you with some easy, practical Endorphin Raising Activities to help you. If we can discipline ourselves to utilize an ERA when we need it, we have conquered the final frontier in staying motivated. Endorphins are motivation's food. Put yourself on an endorphin diet. Be prepared: Doing so could change your life forever.

66 **D**on't measure yourself by what you have accomplished, but rather by what you should have accomplished with your ability. **99**

ANONYMOUS

The Motivation Prescription

66 It's what you
learn after you know it
all that counts. **99**

JOHN WOODEN

By now, I hope you realize that getting and staying motivated is a skill, and one that you have direct control of. It won't be easy, but then again, nothing worthwhile ever is. In this chapter, you will be given your personal prescription for motivation. You will be given fifteen daily doses, each with its own directions. Some doses will take a few days. The prescription will last at least twenty-one (habit forming) days. As with any prescription, follow the directions carefully and do not miss even a single dose. Also, do not go on to the second dose until successfully completing the first dose, and so on. After the initial prescription period, treatment can be maintained by repeating dose fifteen. Remember, the struggle for motivation is ongoing, so stay in the fight daily. This is a win-able battle. Stay committed. Good luck!

DOSE #1

On day one, all that is required is that you spend at least fifteen minutes reflecting on your personal thoughts about motivation. Start by examining which of the motivation myths you might have been guilty of believing. Put your thoughts on paper. Scratch out old limiting beliefs, and write in your new empowering beliefs. Don't just do it in your mind, put it on paper. This is your first treatment.

DOSE #2

For the next two days of your prescription, keep a log tracking the amount of negativity that you are exposed to. Draw a line down the middle of the page. On one side, write positive, the other side, negative. Keep this log with you at all times. Every time either a negative thought comes into your head, or someone else verbalizes something negative, record it in the log. Keep a running tally. Your goal initially should be to have at least as many positive marks as negative. That would translate into a 50 percent positive, 50 percent negative score. Ultimately you should strive for a 80 percent positive reading. You will repeat this dose later in the prescription.

Dose #3

The third dose requires you to go the entire day without blaming, complaining, condemning, or criticizing anyone. This is harder than you think, but totally possible. If necessary, repeat this dose on consecutive days until you have accomplished it.

Dose #4

Start a "Learning Log." Every night, just prior to closing your eyes, write down the single most important thing you've learned that day. This could be a thought, an idea, a skill, or lesson. Number each entry consecutively. In later months and years, your learning log will be more valuable to you than all the notes taken at any seminar you've ever attended. Do not miss even a single entry in your log. Create a cue if needed to help remind you to do it.

Dose #5

The next two days of the prescription requires you to issue at least twenty compliments and twenty thank you's. Do not give more than one at a time. Rapid-fire or insincere compliments and thank you's do not count. This is not as hard as you might expect. When a positive thought comes to mind, verbalize it. Don't analyze how the remark may be taken. If it's genuine, say it. Keep your eye open for places where a compliment is warranted. Same with thank you's. A heart-felt thank you goes further than any gift. Continue to repeat this dose in two-day increments until completion.

Dose #6

Write down your dreams. This dose requires you to find a spot where you can day-dream. Ask yourself the questions from Chapter Five. If your life could be any way you'd like it to be ten years from now, how would it be? Write down your thoughts. Brain storm. You will be asked to organize your thoughts later, but for now, just get them down on paper. Write out every single dream, goal, desire you have. Flush out the ones you are not truly passionate about. Allow at least one hour for this dose. You have the time. It's part of your prescription, for goodness sake!

Dose #7

For the next three days, organize your dreams. First put them in chronological order. Which are short-term dreams, ninety days or less; which are intermediate dreams, within the next two years; and which are long-term dreams, two years or more? Prioritize them. Create a game plan for achieving your dreams. Identify what skills and activities will be necessary during the quest. Be sure, however, to re-think any dream that does not arouse passion when you merely think about it. Also, laugh out loud at least twice during each day of this dose. No reason or stimuli necessary. Matter over mind. Somapsychotics at work!

66   Unless you try to
do something beyond what
you have already mastered,
you will never grow.   99

RONALD OSBORN

Dose #8

Think of and strategically place three cues. Review the chapter on cues if necessary. Make sure your cues truly inspire you. One suggested location is somewhere you can see the cue the second you wake up. Place the other two cues at locations where your motivation tends to wane. Adopt cues as a normal part of your interior decor. They work!

Dose #9

Create your motivation link. Follow the steps exactly for creating a link. Your motivation link is the tool you will use to get motivated in the future, so don't cut any corners. Don't get discouraged if initially your link is not as strong as you might have anticipated. Review Chapter Eight. As with any new skill, it takes practice.

Dose #10

This should be day fourteen of your prescription. But if not, that's ok too. The fact that you've made it this far is no small feat. Pat yourself on the back. Take this day and practice your link. Guide someone else through the process of setting up their own motivation link. This will not only benefit them, but will help solidify the process for you as well.

Dose #11

Create a task link. Think of a task that you have historically been procrastinating. Link a motivating experience to that task. Be sure that the positive feelings of the experience you're using as a recall are stronger than the negative feelings of the task. If not, it won't work. Once you get this procedure down pat, you will want to create a task link for every chore you've put off for years. Now that's motivation!

DOSE #12

Endorphins is the word for the next two days. Engage in at least three ERAs each of the next two days. Make one ERA be to again laugh out loud. Make the laughing sound for one minute. Laughing is magic to the soul. Remember, your mind does not know the difference between faked and real laughter. Hold judgement until you try it. It works. No kidding.

DOSE #13

For the next two days of your prescription, repeat the positive/negative tally log from dose number two. Any increase in the gap between positive and negative means that the medicine is starting to work. If not, you may have either missed a dose or did not follow the directions closely enough. It is suggested that you start over. No big deal. This isn't a race. The positive/negative tally log is your litmus test. Repeat it once a month. If at any time the negative gains on the positive, put yourself back on this prescription. This is one prescription you can write yourself. You're in control.

DOSE #14

You're almost finished. For this dose, perform two unexpected acts of kindness. Expect nothing in return. The joy of giving is

66 The difference between ordinary and extraordinary is a little extra. **99**

ANONYMOUS

your reward. Practice your motivation link a few times as well. Then, just before bed, review your learning log.

Dose #15

The final dose. Read the following "Motivation Affirmation" three times today. You'll find it on an attached card so you won't need to carry this book around with you. One excuse eliminated! After today, read it at least twice every day for the next month. Make it a ritual. Memorize it. After that you can back it down to just once a day. Ok, raise your right hand and repeat after me:

> I choose to be motivated. Motivation is something I control. It may not be easy, but who would expect it to be? I create my own motivation. No holding back. No waiting. No excuses. It is up to me, and that is exciting. I choose a positive life. That is my choice. That is my right. I will watch what I say, for words do come true. I will greet each day with a smile. I will practice somapsychotics when necessary throughout the day. No longer am I powerless to the forces that zap my motivation. I will end the day satisfied and content that I did the best I could. I choose to dream. The only poor people are people who do not dream. With dreams there is hope. With hope there is action. I will not quit on my dreams. Success is a journey, and the rewards are in the journey itself. I choose to stay motivated. Life is more fun when lived with excitement. I know how to stay motivated. It is a skill. It is an art. And it is the choice I make now. This is my life, and it is my decision.

You're On Your Own

This book is not a quick fix. It is, however, intended to be a quick jump start. The results are entirely up to you. You are already motivated, or you wouldn't have bought this book and read it. The decision has been made. Now you just have to act on that decision daily. Remember the great words of Teddy Roosevelt:

> It is not the critic who counts. Not the man who points out how the strong man stumbled, or where the doer of good deeds could have done better. The credit belongs to the man who is actually in the arena, whose face is marred by dust, sweat and blood; who strives valiantly; who errs and comes short again and again; who knows the great enthusiasms, the great devotions, and spends himself in a worthy cause; who at the best, knows the triumph of high achievement; and who, at the worst, if he fails, at least fails while daring greatly, so that his place shall never be with those cold and timid souls who know neither victory nor defeat.

Accept the challenge. Do what it takes. A motivated life is yours for the taking. It's worth the effort.

P.S. Good luck. Learning is a constant, not just reserved for grade school or college. School is in session every day. It is for this reason I end every program the same way. — See you in School . . .

66 **A**ll that matters
is if you can look in the
mirror and honestly
tell the person you see
there that you've
done your best. **99**

JOHN MCKAY

*"Now that I've thought about it,
this motivation stuff could really work!"*

Tips
From
Others

Q.
How do you stay motivated on a daily basis?

I keep going until something good happens, then build on that.

> MIKE STOLL
> COMPANY PRESIDENT

I Love what I do. If you don't, you should learn *to love it.*

> WOLF RINKE, PH.D.
> AUTHOR

I expect the best in others, so it is imperative that I be a positive role model, and example.

> ROBB MULBERGER
> COMPANY PRESIDENT

I think about my goals on a daily, sometimes hourly basis.

> GLORIA GAULT-GEARY
> SEMINAR LEADER

It's less work and less stress to be motivated than to not be motivated. For me, it's a matter of which is harder.

> BRENDA RICHARDS
> HOMEMAKER

Constantly looking forward and not dwelling on past failures.

JASON ABELL
AUTHOR

Talk to friends. Staying connected to those I admire.

LYNNE WAYMON
AUTHOR

Exceeding expectations. Doing what others say can never be done.

TOM ANTION
CORPORATE CONSULTANT

By trying to be a positive influence on other people.

KELLEY MCARTOR
SALESPERSON

I always strive to stay one step ahead of my competition.

KEVIN MCMICHAEL
REAL ESTATE AGENT

I'm my worst critic. The thought of not giving it my all is unacceptable to me. Staying motivated is a necessity.

JOE WALKER .
COMPANY PRESIDENT

By taking care of myself physically. Eating right and exercising keeps my energy level high.

MARGARET KEYS-FOWLER
MANAGER

I actively look for the brand new opportunities that each day brings.

CHARLES F. HELME III
CPA

I work at it. My library is filled with inspirational books and tapes, that I constantly learn from.

STEVEN OCHS
INVENTOR

Believing what I do can make a difference in people's lives.

LIANNE CUMMINGS
PERSONNEL ASSISTANT